EDINBURGH OLD PILGRIMS' WAY

FIRST EDITION
Printed August, 1995

NETHERBOW

Research & text prepared by Donald Smith
Text handwritten & illustrations by John M. Pearson
© Copyright J.M.P. All rights reserved
ISBN 09519134-8-4

Printed by :-
Levenmouth Printers
Banbeath Place
Leven, Fife. KY8 5HD.

EDINBURGH OLD TOWN PILGRIMS' WAY

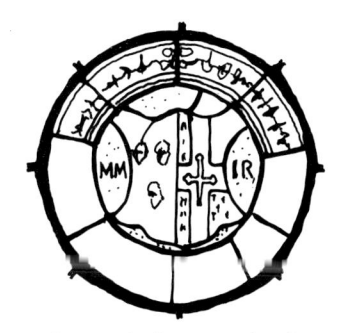

Stained glass window in the Magdalen Chapel.

by Donald Smith & John M. Pearson

St Margaret's Chapel

INTRODUCTION

Scotland's Christian story is everywhere in evidence in historic central Edinburgh. Each phase of national religion has stamped its character on some important building, while in some cases a piece of architecture is all that remains to us of the hopes, fears and pious aspirations of a generation.

Not all of the places on the walks are still places of worship and although some are not open on a daily basis each one may be enjoyed, inside or out and each embodies a distinctive theme in the overall symphony.

The Edinburgh Old Town Pilgrims' Way may be travelled in an afternoon or spaced out over a couple of days. The choice is yours but the invitation to journey through the religious and national experience of Scotland is for everyone who has an eye to see, an ear to hear and a heart and mind to enjoy and understand.

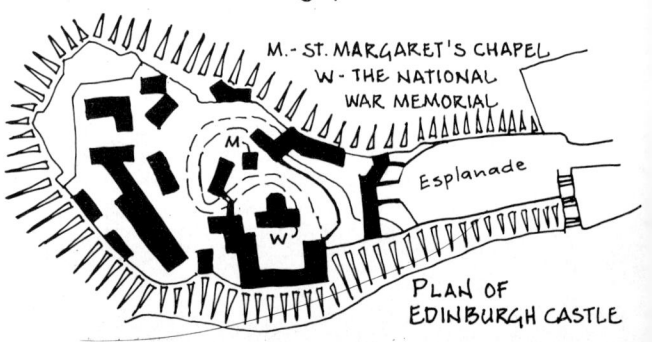

M. - ST. MARGARET'S CHAPEL
W - THE NATIONAL WAR MEMORIAL
Esplanade
PLAN OF EDINBURGH CASTLE

EDINBURGH CASTLE

The cluster of buildings on the Castle rock includes the oldest of Edinburgh's surviving churches. This is surely appropriate since the original settlement must have been concentrated on the fortified rock, but the chapel of St. Margaret with its beautiful miniature Norman arch is a unique jewel.

Margaret, which means pearl, was born an exile in Hungary, daughter of a Saxon prince and a Hungarian princess. When Margaret's father came home to England she was brought up at the court of the pious and learned King Edward the Confessor. There for the first time she met Malcolm of Scotland who had fled from the clutches of Macbeth.

When Edward died without an heir confusion and war followed. The new king, Harold, was killed at Hastings by William the Conqueror. A fugitive once more, Margaret set sail for Hungary but was driven by a storm to the shores of Scotland. Malcolm, now King of Scots came to meet her. He fell in love and asked Margaret to become his queen. Longing for the peace and holy quiet of the cloister Margaret hesitated to marry the warrior king. Then she became Malcolm's wife and Scotland's queen.

From the beginning she opened her arms to the people. Orphans were taken into the Royal Palace, the sick and the suffering tended, prisoners-of-war released and the poor fed.

In Malcolm's eyes Margaret could do no wrong. He supported her work and rewarded those who followed her example. He would take her precious books in his hands turning over the pages and kissing them. Once Malcolm sent for a jeweller to ornament a book with gold and gems, and then he gave it to Margaret as a token of his love. The Royal couple had two daughters and six sons whose upbringing was Margaret's special concern. Margaret also lived a secret life of prayer. From the palace at Dunfermline she would retreat to a cave to be alone with God. At Edinburgh, Malcolm built a chapel for her devotions. This extraordinary Queen lived the ideal of inward glory.

Margaret died in Edinburgh over nine hundred years ago in 1093, shortly after Malcolm's death in battle. Although she worshipped in her own chapel in the castle the existing building was probably built in her memory by her son, David I. Even after nine hundred years the life and personality of Margaret still exert an influence. She remains unique among the universally recognised Scottish Saints in being a woman, and unique among the female Saints worldwide in being a wife and mother.

Stained glass window of St. Margaret in St. Margaret's Chapel.

The National War Memorial

Edinburgh Castle also contains the most important piece of modern religious architecture in Edinburgh. The National War Memorial was well designed by Sir Robert Lorimer and built on the summit of the castle hill between 1924-1927. In many ways it is a restrained and undramatic building but its simple humanity is reinforced by a group of carefully chosen and skilfully executed artistic commissions brought together by Lorimer's guiding hand.

In the shrine itself a bronze frieze runs round the wall depicting the service men and women with a clear graphic line which conveys the hard experience of war without glamorizing or degrading it. The frieze which was designed and executed by Morris and Alice Meredith Williams is like a never ending procession of the lives lost in the horrific waste and destruction of World War One. The stained glass windows by Douglas Strachan are also outstanding and watch out for the little animal sculptures in relief by Phyllis Bone as well as the impressive carving of St. Michael and the many other monuments to each branch of the services. If a visit to Israel should begin at Yad Vashem, the Holocaust Memorial, then perhaps a visit to Scotland ought to include a visit to this memorial which recalls the disproportionate numbers of young Scots who lost their lives in the cause of 'King and country,' in these and other conflicts.

THE HOLY HILL

Below the castle and its esplanade the head of the Royal Mile is dominated by the soaring spire of the Highland Tolbooth Church overtopping a huddle of important ecclesiastical buildings. At first glance this may symbolize spiritual aspiration, but it also embodies Scotland's nineteenth century religious conflicts.

St. John's Highland Tolbooth Church - to give its full title - was originally built to house the General Assembly of the Church of Scotland and its accompanying administrative offices and library. It was designed by Pugin and the Scottish architect Gillespie Graham and built between 1839 and 1844. Pugin's main contribution seems to have been the spire, though the interior is equally striking with a horseshoe plan, built-in pews and an elaborate arrangement of "speaker's throne" and galleries which accommodated the Moderator of the Church's Assembly and the various officials and guests. Outwith the annual assembly the building was used for regular services in Gaelic - hence the Highland connection.

The trouble was that before the building was even complete the Church of Scotland - the majority Protestant and Presbyterian denomination - was riven by a bitter conflict or 'Disruption' which led to the formation of the Free Church of Scotland.

St. John's Highland Tolbooth   St. Columba's-by-the-Castle

Across the land the key institutions of church and school were duplicated in a social division unequalled before or since. On the north side of the High Street the rapidly expanding Free Church built its own theological college to a design by William Playfair and this handsome Gothic building now dominates the Mound as seen from Princes Street below. Between New College and Gillespie Graham's Assembly Hall the Free Church built its own General Assembly Hall.

Since its opening in 1859 the Assembly Hall has been the nearest Scotland has come to a parliament building, with its broad expanse of benches and galleries. When the Church of Scotland and the Free Church (now the United Presbyterian Church) reunited in 1929 the Free Church Assembly Hall was preferred over its established but less roomy rival. When in 1948 Robert Kemp and Tyrone Guthrie were on the hunt for a space in which to stage Scotland's sixteenth century dramatic masterpiece 'Ane Satyre of the Thrie Estaitis' for the Edinburgh International Festival, the Assembly Hall presented itself as the ideal solution giving birth to the thrust stage in contemporary theatre.

Meantime the Assembly Hall of 1844 continued in use as the Highland Tolbooth Church until population drift and secularisation combined to put it out of commission as a church. The latest in a series of proposals for the use of this striking building is that it should become the base of the Edinburgh Festival and perhaps no happier solution could be found to secure the future of this spiritual and cultural treasure.

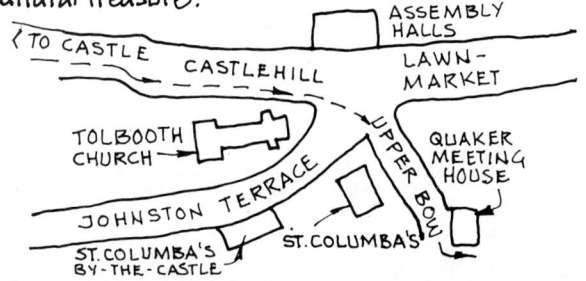

New College from the Mound

When in 1900 the Free Church of Scotland joined with its sister United Presbyterian Church (a product of earlier splits with the Established or Auld Kirk) the way was paved for the great reunion of 1929. However, a minority remained outside each union and in 1900 the continuing Free Church retained St. Columba's Church on the south side of the street as both a church and its General Assembly Hall. It was originally built in 1845 to a design by Thomas Hamilton and traces its roots back to Edinburgh's earliest Gaelic speaking or Highland congregation. In the same year the Scottish Episcopal Church, which was also expanding, built St. Columba's by the Castle a few yards along Johnston Terrace. It began life as an offshoot from Old St. Paul's Episcopal Church further down the High Street. At first the new building was intended to replace the decaying fabric of the Old St. Paul's Meeting House but differences in emphasis over the use of the Scottish Prayer Book and responses to the Oxford Movement led to the continuation of both congregations.

The truly astonishing thing is that all of these buildings were completed within ten years of each other. What must be remembered, however, is that every one of these denominations saw itself as the true heir of the Scottish Reformation inheritance. Sadly Edinburgh's 'Holy Hill' is a monument to Scotland's nineteenth century religious divisions on a grand scale.

St. Columba's Free Church of Scotland

Victoria Street with Victoria Terrace above.

INDEPENDENT ROUTES

To escape the pressure of competing claims to national religion, slip down between the Upper Bow and Free St. Columba's, and on to Victoria Terrace where you will come upon the Quaker Meeting House. The Quakers, or more correctly the Religious Society of Friends, have roots in Scotland reaching back to their own origins in the seventeenth century. Their distinctive style of worship – grounded in silence in which all are equally open to the leading of God – and their steadfast refusal to take oaths or bear arms may have arrived first in Scotland – ironically – with Cromwell's armies. The tradition, however, flourished in a quiet way, producing at least one seminal figure, the theologian Robert Barclay.

The Victoria Terrace Meeting House is a recent development from a former presbyterian building and provides all the facilities of a modern conference or community centre. The upper meeting room commands a dramatic view over the rooftops of the Old Town, and light floods through the tall windows on a clear day. Continuing along Victoria Terrace you emerge onto George IV Bridge and turning right past the National and Central Libraries, you reach two more independent churches.

On the far side is the handsome Augustine Bristo Church which now unites the Scottish Congregational tradition and the United Reformed Church in Scotland. The birth of the Congregational movement in Scotland will always be associated with the famous brothers Robert and James Haldane who were arguably the most successful evangelists in Scotland since Columba and the Celtic Saints. The Church can trace its origins back to that revivalist period in the late eighteenth century though the present building was provided in 1861 for the outstanding Congregationalist preacher Dr. Lindsay Alexander.

The style of the Augustine Bristo Church is a confident blend of Romanesque and classical detail with an ornate tower and spire. Originally a Victorian preaching station the church has adapted to modern conditions by housing the offices of Christian Aid and other important charities on its street frontage and utilising its four storey premises for community activities. Recently the worship area has been restored and upgraded.

On this side of George IV Bridge the Elim Pentecostal Church has carried through an impressive modernisation of a former presbyterian church, which was built in 1859. A wide range of activities for different age groups are provided, all grounded in the church's Evangelical and charismatic ethos. The building is cleverly designed to make maximum use of what is really a corner site, and at the rear on Candlemaker Row it incorporates the site of an earlier Cameronian Meeting House. What these austere Covenanters might make of contemporary charismatic worship must, however, remain speculation.

Augustine Bristo Church

Greyfriars

KIRK OF THE COVENANT

At the end of George IV Bridge cross Candlemaker Row and enter Greyfriars Churchyard. After the Scottish Reformation Edinburgh's Franciscan Friary was transferred by Mary Queen of Scots into the ownership of the Town Council. The city was divided into four parishes and later (1601-20) a new church was built at Greyfriars to serve the south-west area. The design, however, was conservative in style with traditional Gothic features and the stonework of the Convent at Sciennes was recycled so creating an impression of antiquity and continuity.

After many changes the interior of the church has a simple strength and spacious dignity. The timber ceiling, a twentieth century addition, adds warmth and style, while the modern organ and case present an eye-catching contemporary version of late medieval craftsmanship. A careful combination of side pews with loose seating provides maximum flexibility and comfort without disrupting the harmony of this fine interior.

Much of Greyfriars' fame rests with the events to which it has been the silent witness rather than its fabric. In 1638 the National Covenant was signed in the church, marking a complex dispute between Church and State which became entangled in rival systems of church organisation - Presbyterianism versus Episcopacy. Sadly bloodshed ensued and Greyfriars Kirkyard contains a "Martyrs Monument" as well as the remains of the Covenanters' Prison to recall those times of conflict and struggle.

The extraordinary baroque graveyard with its symbolism of scythes, skulls and angels requires an evening to itself, though not by yourself. The rollcall of distinguished names buried here includes George Buchanan and William Robertson among its many churchmen, academics and lawyers. One of Scotland's greatest poets, the Gaelic speaker and writer Duncan Ban MacIntyre is buried here and it was in this kirkyard that Bobby the Skye terrier kept watch over the grave of his master John Grey.

Greyfriars still maintains the tradition of regular services in Gaelic, alongside a liturgical but firmly presbyterian style of worship. In fact Greyfriars has some claim to be the cradle of Scotland's nineteenth century liturgical revival since it was here that the pioneering Robert Lee introduced set prayers, stained glass and an organ for the first time in a Scottish presbyterian church since the austerities of seventeenth century puritanism had replaced Knox's liturgy with an abhorrence of set prayers and read sermons. As so often happens in religion, change comes full circle.

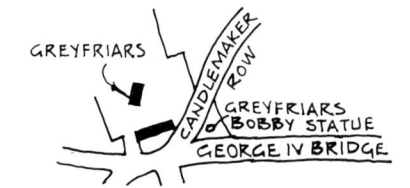

Tolbooth Church spire as seen from Greyfriars

Magdalen Chapel

MAGDALEN CHAPEL

A convenient gate at the foot of Greyfriars Kirkyard could take you out into the Grassmarket but it is usually locked for security. Turn left outside the main entrance and follow Candlemaker Row down into the Grassmarket. In front of you near the opposite end of the pedestrian crossing is the place of public execution where many notable Covenanters met their end. A plaque on the outside of the memorial wall lists the names. As you approach the memorial look up to where Edinburgh Castle looms as a symbol of romantic Scottishness. How must it have seemed to the successive victims of arbitrary power through many generations?

Turning back the way you have come the topography of the Old Town becomes clearer. On the left Victoria Street climbs up towards George IV Bridge and perched above it is the Quaker Meeting House. To the right the Cowgate runs along the foot of the valley separating the Royal Mile and Chambers Street and the Southside on the other. At the mouth of the Cowgate lifting itself above the grime is the delicately aspiring tower of the Magdalen Chapel.

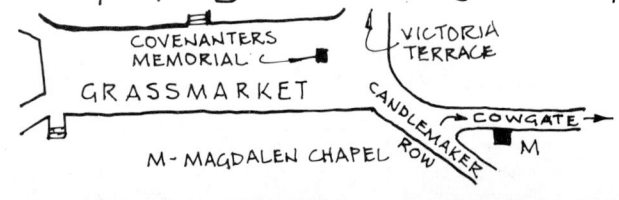

COVENANTERS MEMORIAL
VICTORIA TERRACE
GRASSMARKET
CANDLEMAKER ROW
COWGATE
M - MAGDALEN CHAPEL

Hidden behind a later frontage the Magdalen is a neglected jewel of the medieval era, and one moreover which throws much light on forgotten chapters of Scottish Christianity. The original funds to establish the chapel and its associated hospital or 'home' were left by a pious businessman Michael MacQueen, a prominent member of the Guild of Hammermen, in his will of 1537. The work was completed between 1541 and 1543, only to be succeeded by repairs following the 'Rough Wooing' of Scotland by the earl of Hereford in 1544, and finally confirmed in a Charter of 1547. Substantial funding was supplied by Michael's widow Janet Rhynd, while the inclusion of the royal arms of the Queen Regent in one window suggests that Marie de Guise may also have contributed funds.

But what were they creating and why? The residence was occupied by seven poor 'Bedesmen' or pensioners and a Chaplain. Their job was to look after the Chapel and to conduct daily prayers and regular masses including special prayers for the souls of the deceased, especially the souls of the founders and their relations. This might shorten their inevitable sojourn in purgatory. Apart from this benefit, the endowment of the chapel itself was considered a 'good work' earning merit beyond the grave. This point is reinforced by a text from the Book of Proverbs carved over the Cowgate entrance:
"He that heth Pitie upon the Poore lendeth unto the Lord, and the Lord will recompense him that which he heth given."

The only remaining Pre Reformation stained glass windows left in Scotland.

Inside the chapel the wonderful medieval stained glass roundels with their deep rich colours, and the tomb of Janet Rhynd, remind us of the original purpose of the building. Responsibility for the hospital, however, was handed over to the Guild of Hammermen - note the Hammer and Crown of the Guild with the initials of the founders and the date 1553, also above the door. Soon thereafter came the Reformation when during a period of turmoil the altars and memorial masses were swept away, and the Chapel became the meeting place of the Guild brothers. The present furniture and decoration reflect this use with the tiered seats in the former chancel and the panels recording the donations of Guild members. For over a century the Bedesmen remained in residence but after 1665 the charity was focused on needy members of the extensive Craft and their dependents. The wrought iron screen is itself a demonstration of Craft skills.

15

Stone carving over entrance to the Magdalen Chapel.

Hammer & Crown emblem

Hammer & Crown in the Wrought Iron Screen

Painted craft shield on timber panelling.

16

It is important to stress that religion remained integral to Guild affairs after the Reformation albeit in a changed form. The Bedesmen now said 'Protestant' prayers and as before the adornment of the Chapel served the glory of God and the wellbeing of the Guild in equal measure. In 1620-1625 the handsome steeple was built and a few years later a beautiful silver bell was hung with the inscription (in Latin) :- "Michael Burgherhuis made me to the sole glory of God in 1632" and below this (in Scots) "God bliss the Hammermen of Magdalene Chapel."

The Magdalen Chapel is now owned and cared for by the Scottish Reformation Society and used for occasional worship. This might seem a little surprising for such a typically Catholic medieval foundation, but the first General Assembly of the reformed Church of Scotland met here, on 21st April, 1578 Andrew Melville inaugurated Presbyterianism as the form of Church government, the Second Book of Discipline was debated and John Knox may have been the author of the Hammermens' prayer read at the start of each meeting.

Less gloriously, in later times, the Chapel was used as a post execution mortuary for Covenanters hanged in the Grassmarket and the Earl of Argyll lay here in 1685. It was also used for such miscellaneous activities as the drawing of lotteries (General Assembly take note!) and the exhibition of mechanical curiosities. On its own, however, the Magdalen Chapel is that rare treat an unspoiled and genuine taste of our common heritage.

SAINT GILES CATHEDRAL

Go a little further along the Cowgate and turn left up Old Fishmarket Close and then left again onto the High Street and up to the High Kirk of Edinburgh, the Church of St. Giles.

The Cathedral is the most substantial religious building in the Old Town but it is also one of the hardest to understand. This is because it conceals its own history cladding, layers of experience and evolution in a uniform nineteenth century stone suit. To counteract this tendency fix your gaze firmly on the magnificent Crown Spire which raises an elaborate yet vigorous cantata skywards like a thistle in flower. Now imagine yourself following the tower down to its root, and go without delay in to the centre of the Church underneath the tower.

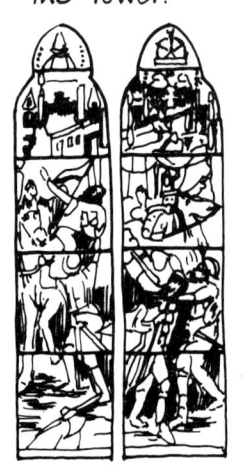

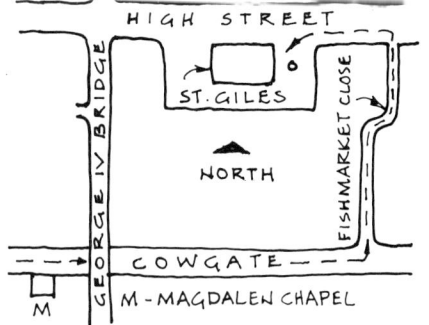

Window in Moray Chapel - Assassination of the Earl of Moray

Crown Spire of St. Giles ▶

You are now at the core of this ancient kirk. Around you are the massive medieval pillars which support the Tower. Looking east you see the sweep of the choir up to the original site of the High Altar. To the west is the nave culminating in the modern Burns Memorial Window, itself a hymn of praise to creation and humanity. To the south is the bold contemporary organ and organ case, and to the north the pulpit and the positions where the Queen and Moderator of the Church of Scotland sit on great occasions of Church and State. On all sides is the dramatic Victorian stained glass, and in the crossing of the medieval church is the Communion Table, the Sacramental heart of Christian worship.

This arrangement is a bold reordering of the traditional long cathedral structure but in the case of St. Giles the concept of a single unified church only dated to the nineteenth century when the sub-division of the building into different churches was reversed in successive phases of restoration. It may be that restoration is a misleading word in this context because, as we shall see, the medieval church itself was a multiple organism with numerous aisles, altars and chapels. This accounts for the remarkable breadth of the church which has four main spaces running east-west as well as two additional 'flanks' of chapels and ancillary rooms. Begin by walking east towards the site of the medieval High Altar, removed at the time of the Reformation in 1560.

Perhaps this is an uncomfortable aspect of the contemporary reordering since something in the building still yearns to face east. Note the ornately carved pillars last in line (the King's Pillar and the Town's Pillar) which mark an extension of the chancel in 1460.

No traces remain but the relics of St. Giles were probably kept here behind the altar in a special shrine. The burgh church of Edinburgh was on this site from at least 1120 and probably earlier but the dedication to Giles, a Greek hermit who settled in France in the seventh century, dates officially to 1243. St. Giles was the Patron Saint of the physically disabled, beggars and lepers, and unsurprisingly popular in these harsh times. The church's greatest period of prosperity, however, followed the presentation of a precious relic, the Saint's armbone, by Preston of Gorton in 1454. The church was granted collegiate status in 1467, coming directly under the authority of the Pope and greatly increasing both its staff of clergy and its appeal to sponsors and benefactors. A new choir and the crown spire followed.

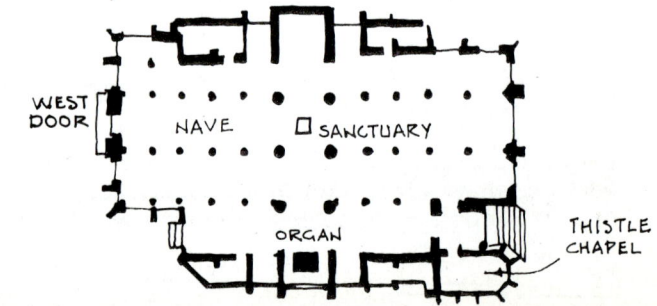

18

St Giles Day is September 1st and was celebrated with a huge procession including the clergy, councillors and guildsmen, harpers, trumpeters and bagpipers. Flowers filled the church and a parade featuring banners, an effigy of the saint, his relics and a garlanded bull went through the town.

The bull, in contrast with the hind which Giles saved in his legend seems a survival from an older fertility rite.

Another survivor from the cult of Giles is the luckenbooth brooch. Originally modelled on two arm bones with interlaced fingers at the top, the popular heart shaped designs were transmuted from pilgrims tokens into love favours. Such was the ingenuity of the gold and silversmiths whose luckenbooths or stalls huddled to the north side of the church, in the face of some small theological difficulties. The last St. Giles procession was held in 1557 and by 1560 the relics were dispersed or destroyed.

If our original approach to the Church of St. Giles suggested a withdrawal or separation of church from world then the time has come to correct that impression for in this case the world was brought into the church. In medieval centuries it was the main public space used for meetings and assignations, business and devotion.

One example of a luckenbooth brooch

The interior was crowded with the chapels and altars of the Trade Guilds and the Confraternities or lay associations, as well as privately endowed chapels. These medieval altars have now been replaced by a rich proliferation of Memorials, most of which date from the nineteenth and twentieth centuries. In between these two great waves of energy, the first civic and second national, lies two largely forgotten centuries of Protestant austerity. Perhaps austerity never fully suited St. Giles or Edinburgh, despite the continuing religious and social influence of its first Protestant Minister, John Knox. Some of Knox's most famous sermons were preached here including his famous attacks on Mary Queen of Scots.

◀ St. Giles

John Knox preaching at the ▲ Funeral of the Earl of Moray.

19

The Sanctuary, looking west.

The chapels and memorials of St. Giles require a book to themselves and a few highlights must suffice. Moving anti-clockwise you pass a modern chapel on the original site of the Chapel of the Holy Cross. Among the plaques here is one to Elsie Inglis the medical pioneer. After the shop entrance you reach the Chambers Aisle or Chapel of Youth, site of the medieval sacristy. William Chambers, the publisher and Lord Provost of Edinburgh was responsible for the heroic labours of the late Victorian restoration. The stone screen in the north transept shows the patron saints of ten of Edinburgh's Trade Guilds, while the Caen stone pulpit (a 19th century addition) depicts six acts of mercy as outlined by Jesus in the parable of the sheep and the goats.

Next in anti-clockwise succession is St. Eloi's Chapel (Patron Saint of the Hammermen and Goldsmiths) now dominated by the Monument to the Earl of Argyll. Then comes St. John's Aisle which is now occupied by an office, and then the Albany aisle now the War Memorial. Albany's original foundation was in expiation of his cruelty in starving the heir to the throne to death in Falkland Palace. Note the elements of fire, air, water and earth around the memorial cross.

John Knox

Skirting round the west door look back to where the statue of John Knox commands the side aisle, and then forward to the Moray Aisle where the Victorians fostered a national corner in imitation of Westminster Abbey. Among the famous faces are David Livingstone, Robert Louis Stevenson, Robert Fergusson and Thomas Chalmers. The Moray Aisle is a conflation of three former chapels but just to confuse the issue the Monument to the Regent Moray (note the magnificent Renaissance brass) is in what remains of the Holy Blude Aisle which belonged to the Guild of Merchants. Moray, who was an illegitimate half brother of Mary Queen of Scots and leader of the Protestant Lords of the Congregation, engineered Mary's deposition but was assassinated in 1570.

Next comes the organ donated by the Salvesen family standing in the south transept, formerly St. Antony's Aisle. Remember to walk round the back of this remarkable instrument. Adjacent to the organ is the Chepman Aisle donated by Edinburgh's first printer in 1513 not long before the Battle of Flodden. Later tragedies are also remembered here with the monument to the Marquis of Montrose executed outside the church in 1650. His gallantry is still commemorated with a rose while his great enemy, Argyll lies on the other side of the church flowerless. A section of the National Covenant is displayed here to remind us of the religious and political issues which brought Scotland decades of strife. Finally, there is the Preston Aisle named after the donor of the famous arm bone.

West Door of St. Giles

From here you can proceed through the glass doors to the Thistle Chapel which was built in 1911 for the Scottish Order of Chivalry after a munificent benefaction for the restoration of Holyrood Abbey, the original home of the order, was judged impractical. The result is an orgy of revivalist craftsmanship masterminded by the architect Robert Lorimer. Compared, however, to his later achievements such as the National War Memorial this is an elaborately contrived hyperbole, overwrought and ultimately claustrophobic. Better to complete your circuit via the Lady Aisle for a last sweeping view of this rugged atmospheric masterpiece in which bold strokes of modern design and colour enliven, but never overcome the intriguing spatial extension and irregularity. The steps here take you to the excellent Lower Aisle cafe passing a monument to the Leprosy Mission - a gentle reminder that St. Giles' good work continues.

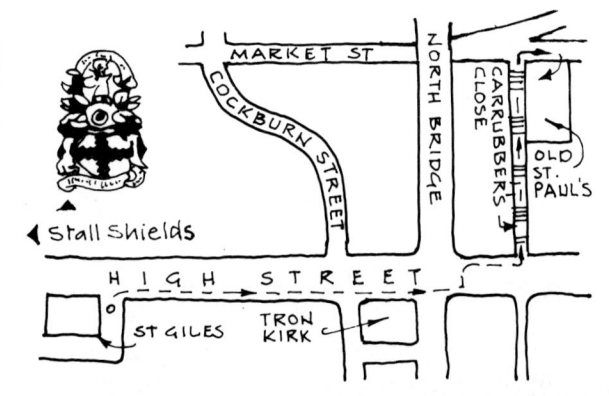

THISTLE CHAPEL

◄ Stall Shields

MARKET ST
COCKBURN STREET
NORTH BRIDGE
CARRUBBERS CLOSE
OLD ST. PAUL'S
HIGH STREET
ST GILES   TRON KIRK

22 Tron Kirk

HIDDEN CHURCHES AND HIGH STREET RELIGION

Going down the High Street from St. Giles you pass the Tron Kirk, another of Edinburgh's post-Reformation burgh kirks. The congregation moved from this site to Moredun, a new area on the south side of Edinburgh, in 1950, paralleling the steady evacuation of Edinburgh's Old Town by the local population which continued until the nineteen eighties. The Tron is now being developed as a tourist information centre for the Old Town. This might come to have a useful function on the Pilgrims' Way since from now on you have to hunt for the Royal Mile's hidden churches.

Cross the busy Bridges at the traffic lights and take Carrubber's Close on the left to reach the secret splendours of Old St. Paul's Episcopal Church. Ascending from the Calvary stair, an impressive 20th century addition, you unfortunately enter from the wrong end since the view from the other end of the church is dramatic. The approach to the high altar is flanked by carved choir stalls and a beautiful rood screen in wrought iron. Seven lamps keep watch over this holy of holies while the altar is surmounted, first by an elaborate golden triptych and then by three long stained-glass lights depicting the Crucifixion, St. Paul and St. Columba. Confined as it is between buildings on both sides, the interior exudes an atmospheric gloom which breathes a sense of sacred mystery.

Old St. Paul's Episcopal Church

23

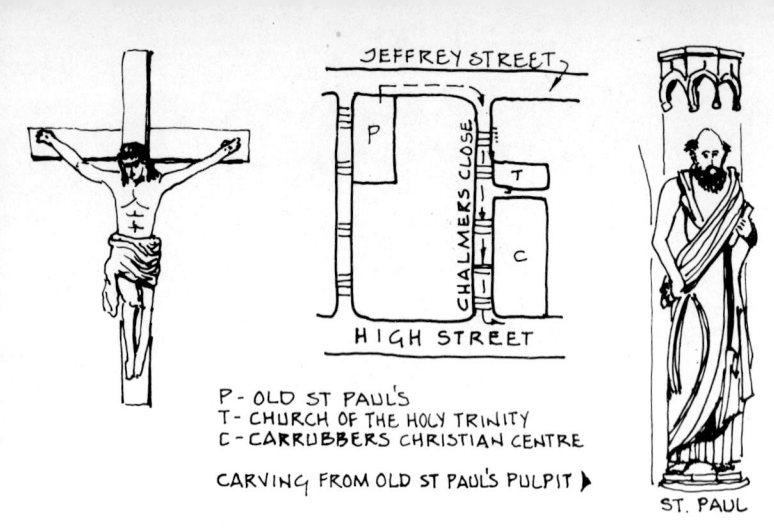

P - OLD ST PAUL'S
T - CHURCH OF THE HOLY TRINITY
C - CARRUBBERS CHRISTIAN CENTRE

CARVING FROM OLD ST PAUL'S PULPIT ▶

ST. PAUL

The history of this intriguing sanctuary is far from straightforward. The present building is a late-Victorian design by Hay and Henderson heavily influenced by the Anglo-Catholic revival or Oxford Movement. The emphasis on liturgy, however, was balanced by a commitment to mission and social action in what had become one of Scotland's worst slum areas, following the withdrawal of the wealthy to the New Town and the influx of Irish immigrants and dispossessed Highlanders. To some extent Old St. Paul's was seen as an 'East End' mission church balancing St. Mary's Episcopal Cathedral in the prosperous West End. To this day Old St. Paul's remains true to these twin inspirations, albeit in changed social and religious circumstances.

But behind this Victorian legacy is an older and to later eyes even more romantic history which adds to the atmosphere of an already remarkable building. When the last Stewart King James VII was deposed in 1689 in favour of the Protestant King William, Presbyterianism was re-established as the sole form of church government, but many Scots continued to support episcopal church government and the Jacobite cause. Under the leadership of Bishop Rose Edinburgh's Episcopalians left St. Giles Cathedral and held services in a wool store in Carrubber's Close - the site of Old St. Paul's Church.

To begin with the Episcopalians represented a broad stream if not a majority viewpoint, but the failure of the Jacobite rebellions of 1715 and 1745, along with the offer of toleration for Episcopalians prepared to swear loyalty to the Hanoverian Kings, reduced the Episcopalian communion to a sad remnant. However, through all these downturns in fortune Old St. Paul's remained stubbornly loyal to its original ethos until in 1789 the Scottish Episcopalians as a whole severed their link with the lost cause of the Stewarts in return for an end to legal discrimination. Even so the mention of George III's name in Old St. Pauls in 1789 produced, in the words of the organist —
"such blowing of noses - such significant hems - such half suppressed sighs - such smothered groans".

These events, of course, took place in a much plainer Episcopalian Meeting House and not in today's revivalist masterpiece. Between the two contrasting buildings lies the steady recovery of Episcopalianism as a distinctive Scottish denomination in the nineteenth century and the Oxford Movement. Yet despite its impeccable native ancestry the Scottish Episcopal Church is regularly described even by some Scots as the Anglican Church in Scotland. The BBC in London can perhaps be forgiven for not knowing better.

Coming back out the main entrance of Old St. Paul's turn right along Jeffrey Street and right again at the hideous modern office block (regular rumours of imminent demolition may be wishful) up Chalmer's Close. Here, you discover the remnants of Mary of Gueldres' magnificent Church of the Holy Trinity (1460). The Church was moved from its original site — which is now covered by Waverley Railway Station — and only the apse survived. Nonetheless something of the grace of this fine medieval church survives along with the original altarpiece — a stunning triptych of the Holy Trinity by the Flemish artist Hugo Van Der Goes, now on display in the National Gallery of Scotland. The apse itself is an excellent brass rubbing centre which is open during the day.

Chapel in Old St. Paul's

Coming up on to the High Street the Carrubbers Christian Centre is immediately on your left, though its refurbished frontage is best seen from the other side of the road. The original mission was founded in 1858 to reach the "unchurched" poor of the Old Town. With a combination of pioneering Sunday Schools and outdoor evangelism meetings, the mission continued to operate from rented premises in Carrubbers Close, until one evening in 1879 their rally was attended by the American evangelist D.L. Moody. "You can't run this mission on air," the redoubtable Dwight is reputed to have said, and he proceeded to launch an appeal for £10,000 to build this Mission Hall. In 1884 he preached the first sermon in its dramatic auditorium, on the text "Come unto me all ye that labour and are heavy laden". Recent renovations have split the old capacious preacher's theatre to provide a range of modern facilities. A striking stained glass image by Fife artist Sandy Parker provides visual focus in the main hall.

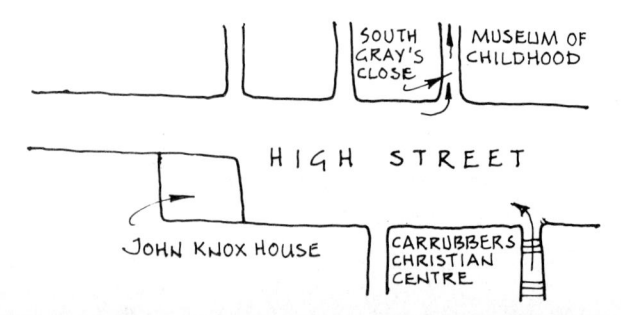

Carrubbers Christian Centre

A few yards further down the High Street on the same side as Carrubbers Centre is the picturesque medieval house associated with John Knox. In fact it is largely the work of a pious Roman Catholic, Mary Queen of Scots goldsmith, Sir James Mossman, who was executed in 1573. The Knox connection remains historically unproven, either way, but certainly saved the house and its equally authentic medieval neighbour from the ravages of the Victorian "improvers." Note the Biblical motto on the frontage and the carved sundial of Moses receiving the Law on Sinai from the Sun or light of God. John Knox House now forms part of the Church of Scotland's Netherbow Arts Centre, and contains an attractive and informative exhibition about the Reformer and the Goldsmith.

Initials of James Mossman & Mariota Arres

LVFE · GOD · ABVFE · AL
AND · YI · NYCHTBOVR
AS · YI · SELF

Moses on Sinai

Mowbray House and John Knox House

27

St. Patrick's Roman Catholic Church

On the other side of the High Street Blackfriars Street retained only the name of a medieval Dominican Friary, but beside the Museum of Childhood, South Grays Close takes you down to St. Patrick's Roman Catholic Church. This building presents two contrasting faces to the world. On the west side, along South Grays, St. Pats is a modest rectangular church with a pleasant treelined forecourt above which rises the shady garden of the presbytery. There is an air of peace and sanctuary here amidst the city centre bustle, and the little portico of the west door lends a gently decorative touch to the solid plainness of the Georgian architecture.

Here in its essentials is the original Episcopalian chapel of 1774, built for those clergy and congregation prepared to swear the oath of allegiance to the Hanoverians. From the Cowgate, however, St. Patrick's presents a much more imposing face with the massive extension of 1929. Here is a sweeping neo-classical arch, statues of St. Patrick and St. Bridget, and a balustrade with curving steps which would do credit to a country mansion. To some extent, however, this is redeemed by an impressive tower with a domed octagonal belfry which is part of the original 1774 design. St. Patrick's was purchased by the Roman Catholic Church in 1856.

Inside, St. Patrick's exhibits its character as the Parish Church of the Old Town's Catholic community. The externally discreet chancel added on the north side in 1898 provides a fitting focus for the liturgy with traditional devotional imagery and statuary. Curiously the original east-west alignment persists through the semi-octagonal apse on the east side which distracts the attention as you enter by the more modest west door. This housed the Episcopalian eucharist and boasts murals by the eighteenth century Scottish artist, Alexander Runciman. However, only these architectural features remain to hint at a hidden past.

With the huge influx of population into the Old Town following the Highland Clearances and the Irish Famines, St. Patrick's became one of the largest Catholic mission churches in Scotland. It is now staffed by Franciscans and can claim connections with two recently beatified Scots, the medieval Franciscan philosopher Duns Scotus and the Blessed Margaret Sinclair who lived in Blackfriars Street earlier in this century.

Looking across the Cowgate you can see the Salvation Army's Hostel for the homeless on the far corner. It is currently being phased out in favour of newer purpose built premises elsewhere. The practical ministry of the Army has been much appreciated in the Old Town since it was first established in the 1880's. The local corps worships in new premises on the Pleasance quite near the Hostel.

CANONGATE TO HOLYROOD

Continue along the last few yards of the Cowgate and turn left up St. Mary's Street which is named after a medieval hospital and chapel. Even the nineteenth century parish hall on the right is now a modern office suite. Look left at the crossroads where John Knox House marks the narrowing (or netherbow) of the High Street towards the medieval port, but turn right into the originally separate Burgh of the Canongate. Keeping on the right hand side you pass a stone cross in the paving marking land once owned by the crusading Knights of St. John. The priory of the modern charitable order is through the archway in St. John's Street alongside the Canongate Kilwinning Masonic Lodge, in which Robert Burns, Scotland's national bard, was enrolled during his stay in Edinburgh.

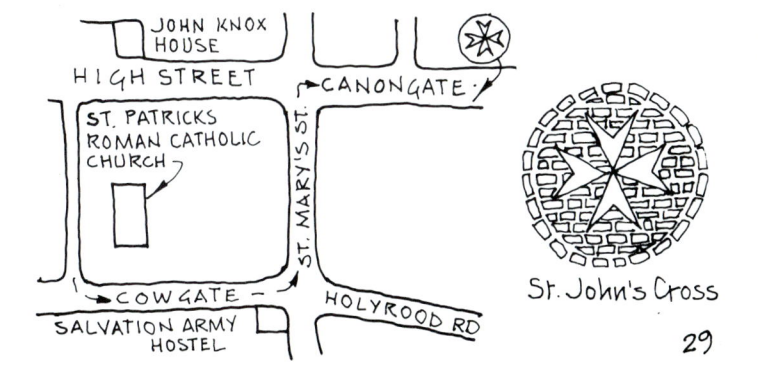

St. John's Cross

29

Proceeding down on the opposite side you come to the Canongate Tolbooth and then the Kirk of the Canongate. This is one of the most famous church gables in Scotland and its handsome curves, neatly offset by the Doric portico, have been initiated in other buildings. The portico is surmounted by the arms of Thomas Moodie whose 'mortification' or legacy funded the building in 1688-91, and by the royal arms above the round window.

The royal connection is important since it was James VII's decision to convert the nave of Holyrood Abbey into a chapel for the Order of the Thistle that led to the building of the church. Ironically James' own reign was cut short two years later and the Abbey was irretrievably damaged by an anti-popery riot, leaving the Canongate Kirk to take root in the impeccably Presbyterian era of William of Orange. Despite this it has been suggested that James Smith's design of an aisled three bay nave with shallow transepts and a capacious chancel was deliberately adaptable for Roman Catholic worship had the Revolution of 1689 not intervened.

Enter the main door noting the recent engraved glass doors by John Laurie. The vestibule contains an interesting 18th century Benefaction Board and photographs of recent royal visits, but these can be viewed later.

Kirk of the Canongate

The effect on entering the church is of light filling strong plain volumes of space. This is partly due to the absence of stained glass and partly to the dominant light colours of woodwork and walls, but the church's most formative feature is perhaps its high arches and vaults all evincing solidity and harmonious order. The chancel window looks out onto Calton Hill, and the former Royal High School, the designated parliament building of a nation without a parliament. Walking down the central aisle you get the full play of light and space, while looking back the gable window sheds further illumination over the gallery front with its painted emblems of the Trades Guilds.

The present furnishings and layout of Canongate Church are largely twentieth century and owe their inspiration to the liturgical revival in the Church of Scotland of which the Canongate's ministers have been leading lights. Parish worship each Sunday is based on John Knox's Book of Common Order and the nave pulpit, prayer desks, apse and main pulpit (once used by Thomas Chalmers) are all brought into play.

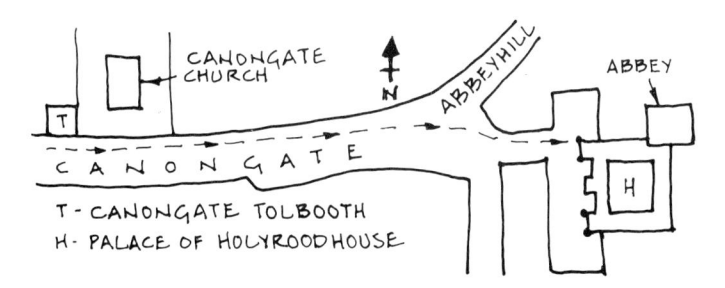

T - CANONGATE TOLBOOTH
H - PALACE OF HOLYROODHOUSE

BAXTERS

Guild Emblems

CORDINERS

31

1. Arms of 'Governor of the Castle'.
2. Arms of 'Captain General of the Bodyguard'.
3. Adam Smith's grave.
4. Carving on monument to soldiers who died in the Castle from 1692-1880.

To your left the transept houses a War Memorial Chapel (look out for the tiny carved figure of St. Michael above the entrance) while to the right St. David's Aisle recalls the church's Holyrood ancestry and the Royal Scots. The painting is by Stanley Cursiter and the wall mounted glass panel from the regiment's former chapel in Germany. At the front of the nave the royal pew and the pew of the Governor of Edinburgh Castle emphasize the church's additional roles as a garrison church and as the Parish kirk of the Palace of Holyroodhouse.

Carving on Coach Driver's Tombstone

The kirk yard requires another visit in its own right. Among other famous names it includes the last resting place of Adam Smith, author of "The Wealth of Nations" and founder of modern economics, as well as the touching headstone set up by Robert Burns in 1789 for his fellow poet Robert Fergusson who died tragically in Edinburgh's bedlam.

"No sculptur'd Marble here nor pompous lay
 No storied Urn nor animated Bust
 This simple stone directs Pale Scotia's way
 To pour her sorrows o'er her Poet's Dust."

All in all this remarkable seventeenth century church breathes the spirit of Scotland's eighteenth century culture in a way unmatched by any later building.

ROYAL RELIGION

The last building on the Pilgrims' Way is like the first, an expression of the devotion of David I of Scotland and of his reverence for his mother Queen Margaret. Holyrood Abbey was founded by David for the Augustinian Canons in 1128 and probably took its name from a holy relic - a fragment of the True Cross - treasured by St. Margaret. Nonetheless romance, not entirely discouraged by David himself, embellished the foundation with the legend of David's encounter in the royal hunting park with an enraged stag. Thrown from his horse the King was pinned to the ground but on trying to grab hold of the antlers David found himself grasping a crucifix. The stag withdrew and that night in a dream David was commanded to "make a house for canons devoted to the Cross" - hence the Canongate. These events took place conveniently on the Feast of Exaltation of the Holy Cross, and Stanley Cursiter's oil painting in the Canongate Church catches something of their dreamlike spiritual quality.

Whatever its origin Holyrood Abbey was to become one of the most important medieval monasteries in Scotland and later, also a royal residence which is the principal function of the site today. Only the ruined nave of the Abbey remains but even in its diminished state it hints at something of the richness and beauty of the Abbey church.

Holyrood Abbey

Note the beautiful arcading in the north aisle, the Romanesque door in the south-east corner which led to the cloister and which survives from David's first church; and the still magnificent west front which evolved over centuries, with tiers of decorative arcading, twin towers and an elaborate processional doorway.

Unfortunately Holyrood was very vulnerable to attack and suffered from successive English invasions including the 'rough wooing' of 1544 which carried off the Abbey's brass eagle lectern. From all of these depradations, however, the Abbey recovered, and even after the Reformation the nave continued in use as the Parish church. Finally in a strange echo of John Knox's dispute with Mary Queen of Scots over worship at the palace an Edinburgh mob wrecked the Abbey church in protest at James VII's perceived intention to restore Catholicism, and his removal of the parish congregation beyond the palace precincts. A last botched repair resulted in a roof collapse and the ruin which stands today.

For all that, this is still a place of beauty and inspiration, inviting quiet reflection on the vanity of all passing forms of religion, contrasted with the enduring pilgrimage of Christian faith through the centuries.

THE END

West front, Holyrood Abbey.

ILLUSTRATIONS

4. St. Margaret's Chapel
5. Stained glass window in the Chapel
6. The National War Memorial
7. St. John's Highland Tolbooth and St. Columba's by-the-Castle.
8. New College
9. St. Columba's Free Church of Scotland
10. Quaker Meeting House - Victoria Terrace
11. Augustine Bristo Church.
12. Greyfriars
13. Highland Tolbooth from Greyfriars
14. Magdalen Chapel
15. Stained glass windows in the Chapel
16. Emblems and crests of the Hammermen
17. Crown spire of St. Giles
18. Plan of St. Giles
19. St. Giles, John Knox, luckenbooth brooch
20. Sanctuary, St. Giles
21. West Door of St. Giles
22. Tron Kirk
23. Old St. Paul's Episcopal Church.
24. St. Paul
25. Chapel in Old St. Paul's
26. Carrubbers Christian Centre
27. Mowbray House and John Knox House
28. St. Patricks Roman Catholic Church
29. St. John's Cross
30. Kirk of the Canongate
31. Guild shields, coat-of-arms, clock
32. Adam Smith's grave and other tombstones.
33/34. Holyrood Abbey
35. Elim Pentecostal Church
36. St. Giles

CONTENTS

4. Introduction
7. The Holy Hill
10. Independent Routes
12. Kirk of the Covenant
14. Magdalen Chapel
17. St. Giles Cathedral
22. Hidden Churches and High Street Religion
29. Canongate to Holyrood
33. Royal Religion

Heraldic Stall Shield in the Thistle Chapel, St. Giles.

Elim Pentecostal Church

ACKNOWLEDGEMENTS

With thanks to Robert Hamilton for help with research, Duncan Smith and Kay Shanks for help with the word-processing, and Alison for patience.

St. Giles Cathedral

Guild shield - Canongate Kirk

Brass Rubbing Centre Motif

Stained glass window in the Magdalen Chapel.

Bible Land - Canongate

Donald Smith is Director of the Netherbow Arts Centre and Curator of John Knox House on Edinburgh's Royal Mile. He has published a number of books and articles on the culture and religion of Scotland, and is also an active playwright and theatre director. He is a graduate of Edinburgh University and holds a doctorate in Scottish Literature from the University's School of Scottish Studies.

John Pearson is an architect having graduated with a Bachelor of Architecture degree at Heriot-Watt University in 1976. In recent years he has published several books of local and historical interest on Fife, Edinburgh, Stirling and Inverness. He travelled overseas between 1977-1983, and then worked for Edinburgh architects' firm Dick Peddie & McKay, at their branch office in Invergordon, until 1987. Following a six year spell in London he is now based at Perth working on a freelance basis.

Other Publications by John M. Pearson

A Guided Walk round Inverness
A Guided Walk round St. Andrews
A Guided Walk round Edinburgh
Burntisland
Three part series on Kingdom of Fife :-
"Around North East Fife
Around Kirkcaldy
Around Dunfermline."
Around Stirling.   (tel. 01333 426248)

36